TOOLS FOR TEACHERS

- **ATOS:** 0.6
- **GRL:** A
- **LEXILE:** 20L

- **CURRICULUM CONNECTIONS:** opposites, sorting
- **WORD COUNT:** 64

Skills to Teach

- **HIGH-FREQUENCY WORDS:** a, be, can, what
- **CONTENT WORDS:** clothes, dog, land, paint, slide, street
- **PUNCTUATION:** periods, question marks
- **WORD STUDY:** initial *s*-blends (*slide, street*); long /i/, spelled *y* (*dry*), *i_e* (*slide*); long /a/, spelled *ai* (*paint*)
- **TEXT TYPE:** compare/contrast

Before Reading Activities

- Read the title and give a simple statement of the main idea.
- Have students "walk" though the book and talk about what they see in the pictures.
- Introduce new vocabulary by having students predict the first letter and locate the word in the text.
- Discuss any unfamiliar concepts that are in the text.

After Reading Activities

Write the book's language pattern on the board: "(A)_____can be wet." in one column, and "(A)_____can be dry." in another. Encourage children to think about things that are wet and things that are dry, as well as things that can be both wet and dry. Write their answers under the appropriate column.

Tadpole Books are published by Jump!, 5357 Penn Avenue South, Minneapolis, MN 55419, www.jumplibrary.com

Copyright ©2018 Jump. International copyright reserved in all countries. No part of this book may be reproduced in any form without written permission from the publisher.

Editor: Jenny Fretland VanVoorst **Designer:** Anna Peterson

Photo Credits: Dreamstime: Anastasiia Prokofyeva, cover; Anna Utekhina, cover; Cwastudios, 6. Getty: Miguel Sotomayor, 9; Blue Jean Images, 14, 14-15. Shutterstock: Svitlana-ua, 1; Levente Fazakas, 2-3; Melica, 3; KristinaSh, 4; Konstantin Gushcha, 5; IgorAleks, 7; Romrodphoto, 8, NadyaEugene, 8; WATHIT H, 10; Zack Frank, 11; TravnikovStudio, 12; wk1003mike, 13.

Library of Congress Cataloging-in-Publication Data
Names: Donner, Erica, author.
Title: Wet and dry / by Erica Donner.
Description: Minneapolis, MN: Jump!, Inc., (2017) | Series: Opposites | Audience: Ages 3-6. | Includes index.
Identifiers: LCCN 2016058409 (print) | LCCN 2017004772 (ebook) | ISBN 9781620317556 (hardcover: alk. paper) | ISBN 9781620317754 (pbk.) | ISBN 9781624966026 (ebook)
Subjects: LCSH: Water—Juvenile literature. | Evaporation—Juvenile literature. | English language—Synonyms and antonyms—Juvenile literature. | Polarity—Juvenile literature.
Classification: LCC QC920 .D596 2017 (print) | LCC QC920 (ebook) | DDC 428.1—dc23
LC record available at https://lccn.loc.gov/2016058409

OPPOSITES

WET AND DRY

by Erica Donner

TABLE OF CONTENTS

tadpole
books

WET AND DRY

Paint can be wet.

Paint can be dry.

A dog can be wet.

A dog can be dry.

Clothes can be wet.

clothes

Clothes can be dry.

A street can be wet.

A street can be dry.

Land can be wet.

Land can be dry.

A slide can be wet.

slide ·····▶

A slide can be dry.

What else can be wet?

What else can be dry?

WORDS TO KNOW

clothes

dog

land

paint

slide

street

INDEX